Cooper Thomas

Letters on the Slave Trade

First Published in Wheeler's Manchester Chronicle and Since Re-Printed

with Additions and Alterations

Cooper Thomas

Letters on the Slave Trade
First Published in Wheeler's Manchester Chronicle and Since Re-Printed with
Additions and Alterations

ISBN/EAN: 9783337201548

Printed in Europe, USA, Canada, Australia, Japan

Cover: Foto ©ninafisch / pixelio.de

More available books at **www.hansebooks.com**

PREFACE.

THE following pages contain the substance of four Letters on the Slave Trade, which I wrote for the purpose of contributing my mite of Information, upon a subject of importance, to the Inhabitants of Manchester. They appear to have excited some attention; and at the request of some Gentlemen, who very laudably interested themselves in favour of the wretched Africans, they are now reprinted, for the purpose of being dispersed gratis. Every man condemns the Trade in general; but it requires the exhibition of particular instances of the enormity of this Commerce, to induce those to become active in the matter, who wish well to the cause upon the whole. I have not thought it necessary to preserve the epistolary form exactly agreeable to the original stile of publication; because the omission of the proems and conclusions of the letters, have made room for more important matter. I fancy the reader, if his leisure will not enable him to attend to the minutiæ of the subject, will find in this Pamphlet facts sufficient to form a decided opinion upon the question. If he have leisure, I hope he will hereby be induced to enter more deeply into the investigation, for I am sure the cause of Humanity will be assisted by every one who pays a sufficient attention to the Commerce here reprobated.

THOMAS COOPER.

Woodbeys, near Altringham,
  Cheshire, Oct. 1787.

It is to be hoped that those who receive any Copies of this Pamphlet, will distribute them in conformity to the design of the publication.

A

T O

TO THE PRINTER OF THE MANCHESTER CHRONICLE.

S I R,

Quid non mortalia pectora cogis
Auri sacra fames?

THE public attention is so frequently excited, by exagge
rated representations of evils, which extend not beyond
the limits of a family, or the person of the relator; by mis-
fortunes of diurnal occurrence, or the speculations of fictious
distress; and we are so frequently addressed by the self-devoted
victims of negligence or misconduct, and by those who spurn
at the laws which Humanity has dictated for the relief of the
necessitous, that some attention may reasonably be expected,
to the narration of miseries which *cannot* be exaggerated;
which extend to millions of our fellow-creatures; which are
induced by no delinquency of the sufferers; are increased and
authorised, not alleviated, by laws, which avarice and oppression have enacted and enforced, against the wretched, but
innocent, objects of their legislative authority.

But it is not solely on the score of humanity, that the public may be addressed on the present occasion: if it be our boast
as Englishmen, that we (as all men ought to be) are governed
by these laws only to which we have an opportunity of assent-
ing; if we claim Freedom as our birth-right, and glory that
the "very air of our country is too free for a slave to respire;"
we are in honour bound to assist in exterminating the most dia-
bolical exertion of political tyranny, which the annals of
oppression can exhibit an instance of.

As honest and religious men, as Christians, followers of that
Master whose life was *Benevolence*, whose name is *Love*, how
can we do otherwise than discountenance a practice, which in-
volves almost every vice that fills the black catalogue of human
iniquity, and wherein fraud, perjury, and cruelty, attend as
the handmaids of commercial avarice.

What this practice is, the reader has already conjectured—
for to what is this language applicable, but to the infamous
traffic of the human Species—the A F R I C A N   S L A V E
T R A D E.

Every

Every man poffeffed of the common feelings of humanity, and the common principles of morality, even if unacquainted with the particulars of this execrable commerce, mentions it in difcourfe in terms of difapprobation, and hears it with an ejaculation of abhorrence. But the miferies of five hundred thoufand wretches, noticed in general terms, feldom produces a permanent effect among perfons, who would fhudder at the detail of the complicated mifery, which any individual of the ill-fated group has been doomed to undergo.

It is *particular* diftrefs, with its attendant circumftances, which is calculated to excite compaffion. A general carnage is feldom mentioned with pain, and is always heard without a tear. Happily for the human fpecies, fuch is the cafe: for otherwife, either human nature would prefently fink under the agony of perpetual fympathy, or the nobleft feelings which Heaven has beftowed on mankind, would be foon extinguifhed by repeated exertion.

That fome very few circumftances, however, attending this inhuman traffic, may be generally known to the Readers of your Paper, I have drawn up (principally in the words of the relators) a very brief account of the hiftory of this commerce; of the writers who have exprefsly complained of it; of the mode of procuring the flaves; of the labour they are doomed to exert; and of the general treatment they receive from their Chriftian mafters. In this account I fhall be careful not to infert any thing which writers of repute have not ventured their credit on, or which is not fufficiently and literally notorious, to every perfon who has poffeffed an opportunity of feeing or hearing the facts in queftion. Exaggeration in the flighteft degree is fo perfectly needlefs, that it fhall not be attempted. Even thofe who relate much lefs than the truth, have great rea-fon to fear their readers will fufpect them of telling much more.

It is well known, that in the early ages of the world cap-tives were led into perpetual fervitude, whofe mafters confi-dered themfelves entitled to vend them. This practice conti-nued throughout Greece, obtained among the Romans, and was in ufe among all the Barbarians, who overturned the Ro-man Empire, and fubftituted the Feudal Syftem in the place of Roman Jurifprudence. From the excellent and accurate com-pilations of Wright, Gilbert, Blackftone, and Robertfon, the *Villeins* of the Feudal times appear to have been true flaves; whofe perfons, families, and poffeffions, were the property of the lord of the foil; but whofe treatment, though harfh, was comparatively merciful: the practice, however, of continuing

A 2 our

our fellow-creatures in a ftate of fuch extreme fubordination, and regarding and treating them fo much like the cattle of the field, rather than as beings of the fame fpecies with their own-ers, was fo utterly repugnant to the benignant genius of Chriftianity, even in thofe dark ages, that the Clergy univer-fally fet their faces againft it, with fo much zeal and fo much fuccefs, that toward the clofe of the 12th century, the clafs of people termed Villeins hardly exifted throughout Europe.

About the clofe of the 15th century, however, the idlenefs and inhumanity of the Portuguefe incited them to commit de-predations on the African coaft, with the intent of carrying the natives to cultivate their newly difcovered American fettle-ments. The Spaniards having nearly exterminated the Ame-rican Indians in the Continent they poffeffed, followed the example of the Portuguefe—not without the approbation and incitement of Bartholomew de la Cafas, who was blind to the rights of human nature in one part of the world, while he was fpending his life in maintaining them in another. The com-merce then fell into the hands of the Genoefe, and by degrees the Englifh, the French, the Dutch, and the Danes fhared in the bloody traffic. The Englifh, however, foon became, and ftill continue pre-eminent in wickednefs: the fupply of their own colonies before the war requiring the annual increafe of nearly 100,000 of thefe unfortunate victims of indolence and avarice.

This fpecies of barter, however, has not been practifed en-tirely without reprehenfion. The Africans found an advocate in the laft century, in a Britifh Clergyman of the name of *Morgan Godwyn*. But of all others they are the moft indebted to that moft refpectable of religious denominations, the Quakers. *John Woolman* and *Anthony Benezet*, Members of that fect, about the middle of the prefent century, fpent a great part of their lives and fortunes in the attempt to abolifh, among the people of their own perfuafion, a practice fo tho-roughly inconfiftent with every principle of common honefty, and every precept of every religion. Their endeavours were not totally unfuccefsful; for this traffic, which had been no-ticed with reprehenfion by the Quakers in 1727, was publicly condemned at their yearly conference in 1754, wherein they declared, " that to live in eafe and plenty by the toil of thofe whom fraud and violence had put into their power, was neither confiftent with Chriftianity, nor common juftice." Thefe fentiments, publicly perfifted in from that time to the prefent by that refpectable body, has had no fmall weight; for throughout the Continent of North America, there is not

at

at this day a single slave, in the possession of an acknowledged Quaker. The example of the Quakers induced other sects in America to consider the admissibility of slaves among their respective members. Among the Presbyterians in Pensylvania, I am sorry to say the question respecting the universal manumission of slaves was negatived, though but by a majority of one.

In the year 1774 the Rev. Mr. J. Wesley, with that active benevolence that has perpetually marked his character, took into consideration this subject, in a pamphlet entitled " Thoughts on Slavery." This tract, written with the author's usual con ҃ cisenefs, and which for importance of fact, for cogency of argument, and for neatness of stile has not been exceeded by any writer upon this subject, so well displays the impropriety of the traffic, that little else would be necessary than to reprint and disperse it, if the unblushing denials of notorious facts by some late hirelings of Slavery, did not call for additional instances of British inhumanity.

Several tracts on this subject have also been published by Mr. Grenville Sharp, who, to his immortal honour, at his own expence, procured the perpetual manumission of slaves in England, by means of the decision in the great cause of *Somerset* the negro. And I confess I think a different decision could hardly be given, if a similar cause, after being carried through the inferior courts in the plantations, were regularly removed for a final discussion to this country.

Next to the unremitting representations of the Quakers, however, the public attention has been principally excited by the Rev. Mr. James Ramsay's " Essay on the Treatment and Conversion of African Slaves," and the controversy to which it gave rise. A controversy wherein the anonymous antagonists of humanity have been so completely foiled, and Mr. Ramsay's facts so thoroughly established, (by the concurrent testimony of Capt. J. Smith in particular) that it will be difficult for them to escape the accusation of gross calumny and wilful misrepresentation. Mr. Ramsay's publication was succeeded by a Translation of a Latin Dissertation " on the Slavery and Commerce of the Human Species;" for which the author, (the Rev. Mr. Clarkson) was deservedly honoured with the first prize by the University of Cambridge, in the year 1785. This elaborate essay is a full and compleat discussion of the subject, and exhibits new facts and additional authorities. I am happy to say that the learned and excellent author is yet employed in collecting and arranging with unremitted industry, materials for farther public information on this important subject. If to
these

thefe be added the authors mentioned in the reference,* the catalogue will be nearly complete, of thofe who have thus honourably, and, I hope, not ufelefsly employed their leifure hours.

The publications, however, on this fubject, are not fo much known as they deferve : they are alfo too numerous to be properly attended to by thofe who have not leifure to read much, and who have no inducement to pay for information of which they know not the importance.

It has occurred to me, therefore, that it would conduce to the furtherance of a Caufe which deferves all manner of fupport, if I were to felect and make known fuch facts, properly authenticated, concerning the methods of procuring flaves, the tafks they are bound to perform, and the general treatment to which they are fubject, as will fhew the extent of the evil complained of, and juftify the charges which the Writers above enumerated have brought againft the traffic in queftion.

At the firft vifits of the Portuguefe and other European nations to the Coaft of Africa, they feized without fcruple fuch of the natives as they found, and carried them into fervitude to their American Colonies. But this practice could not laft long : the Africans deferted the fea coaft; they were followed up the rivers and creeks; the banks of thefe became deferted in their turn, and the trade was on the decline. The only alternative was to make fettlements on the coaft, and obtain by purchafe, what they could not procure by force. This was done; and in the year 1481 the firft European Fort was erected by the Portuguefe at *D'Elmina.* When by change of conduct in the Europeans,

---

* The prefent excellent Bifhop of Chefter, in a Sermon preached before the Society for propagating the Gofpel in foreign parts, recommends to their confideration, the prefent State of the enflaved Africans. Much to his Lordfhip's honour, he is the firft clergyman of the Eftablifhment, who has profeffionally taken up the caufe. So fair an example, it is to be hoped, will be univerfally followed.

The fubject has alfo been exprefsly treated by T. Day, Efq. in a Pamphlet entitled "Fragments on Negro Slavery."

The author of a Serious Addrefs to the Rulers of America, on Slavery.

The cafe of the opprefsed Africans, by the Quakers.

Capt. Smith's Letter, to the Rev. Mr. Hill, on the State of the Negro Slaves.

Thoughts on the Slavery of the Negroes. 2nd. Edit.

The dying Negro, a Poem.

Weft-Indian Eclogues.

The Wrongs of Africa, a Poem. This laft is of confiderable merit : nor are the others ill written.

Thefe, with the publications of the writers mentioned in the letter, amount in number to 18 or 20.

peans, an intercourse was establifhed between them and the Africans; the former agreed for the purchafe, 1. of convi&s fentenced to death; 2. of prifoners of war: but the demand was fo great on the one fide, and the traffic fo lucrative on the other, that altho' throughout the whole of the Slave coaft where the wants of the Europeans were known, every crime, every mifdemeanour, nay every fufpicion of a crime was made capital to increafe the fupply, the demand was ftill infatiate; and the traders recurred to the purchafe, 3dly. of natives feized in profound peace by the abfolute authority of the Prince; and 4thly. of natives kidnapped by thofe who now began to make a trade of it. Such are the fources from whence the demand has now, for nearly three centuries, been fupplied.

That fuch is the cafe, is notorious: but a better idea of this commerce will be formed from the fubfequent accounts which I have felc&ed from the Authors quoted.

About the year 1551 the Englifh firft began to trade to the Coaft of Guinea. In 1566 Sir John Hawkins failed with two fhips to Cape Verd, where he fet 80 men on fhore *to catch negroes.* But the natives flying, he fell farther down, and there fet the men on fhore, *to burn their towns, and take their inhabitants.* But they met with fuch refiftance, that they had feven men killed, and took but ten negroes. So they went ftill farther down, till having taken enough, they proceeded to the Weft Indies, and fold them.[*]

"When the King of Barfalli (fays Mr. Moore, who was fa&or to the African Company in 1730) wants goods or brandy, he fends to the Englifh Governor at James Fort, who immediately fends a floop. Againft the time it arrives, he plunders fome of his neighbours' towns, felling the people for the goods he wants. At other times he falls upon one of his own towns, making bold to fell his own fubje&s."

The French get their flaves much in the fame way. "I wrote (fays *Monf. Brue)* to the King, if he had a fufficient number of flaves, I would treat with him. He feized 300 of his own people, and fent word he was ready to deliver them for the goods." Monf. *Barbot,* another French fa&or, fays, "Many of the flaves fold by the negroes are prifoners of war, or taken in the incurfions they make into the enemy's territories; others are ftolen. Abundance of little blacks of both fexes are ftolen away by their neighbours, when found abroad on the road, or in

---

[*] This was the commencement of the *Englifh* Slave Trade, and in dire& contradi&ion to the exprefs orders of Queen Elizabeth, as appears from Hill's naval hiftory, page 296.

in the woods, or else in the corn fields, at the time of year when their parents keep them there all day, to scare away the devouring birds."

To set the manner wherein negroes are procured in a yet stronger light, it will suffice to give an extract of two voyages to Guinea on that account. The first is taken verbatim from the original manuscript of the Surgeon's journal.——"Sestro, Dec. 29, 1724. No trade to day, tho' many traders came on board. They informed us that the people are gone to war within land, and will bring prisoners enough in two or three days, in hopes of which we stay.

"The 30th. No trade yet: but our traders came on board to day, and informed us the people had burnt four towns; so that to-morrow we expect slaves off.

"The 31st. Fair weather, but no trading yet. We see each night towns burning, but we hear many of the *Sestro* men are killed by the inland negroes; so that we fear this war will be unsuccessful.

"The 2d. Jan. Last night we saw a prodigious fire break out about 11 o'clock—and this morning see the town of *Sestro* burnt down to the ground. (It contained about 100 houses.) So that we find their enemies are too hard for them at present, and consequently our trade spoiled here. Therefore about seven o'clock we weighed anchor, to proceed lower down."

The second extract taken from the journal of a Surgeon, who went from New-York on the same trade, is as follows. "The commander of the vessel sent to acquaint the King that he wanted a cargo of slaves. The King promised to furnish him, and in order to it, set out, designing to surprize some town, and make all the people prisoners. Some time after, the King sent him word he had not met with the desired success, having attempted to break up two towns, and having been twice repulsed; but that he still hoped to procure the number of slaves. In this design he persisted till he met his enemies in the field. A battle was fought which lasted three days, and the engagement was so bloody, that 4500 men were slain upon the spot." Such is the manner wherein the negroes are procured; and thus *Christians* preach the Gospel to the *Heathens!* exclaims the Rev. Mr. Wesley, from whose " Thoughts on Slavery," the preceding extracts are made.—The facts are from Benezet.

The foregoing transcripts justify the observations of Mr. *Clarkson*, from whose " Essay on the Slavery and Commerce of the Human Species," p. 97, et seq. I have taken the following very melancholy account.

Whoever

Whoever reflects on the prodigious slaughter that is constantly made in every African skirmish, will find that where 10 are taken, he has every reason to presume that 100 perish. In some of these skirmishes, though they have been begun for the express purpose of *procuring slaves*, the conquerors have suffered but few of the vanquished to escape the fury of the sword: and there have not been wanting instances, where they have been so incensed at the resistance they have found, that their spirit of vengeance has entirely got the better of their avarice, and they have murdered in cool blood every individual, without discrimination either of age or sex. The following is an account of one of these skirmishes, as described by a person who was witness to the scene; who was known to Mr. Clarkson himself, and who having been shipwrecked on the African coast, resided a considerable time among the natives. The subsequent account is a transcript from his letter.———"I was sent with several others in a small sloop up the river Niger, to purchase slaves. We had some free negroes with us in the practice: and as the vessels are liable to frequent attacks, from the Negroes on one side of the river, or the Moors on the other, they are all armed. As we rode at anchor a long way up the river, we observed a large number of negroes in huts by the river side, and for our own safety kept a wary eye on them. Early next morning we saw from our mast-head, a numerous body approaching, with apparently but little order, but in close array. They approached very fast, and fell furiously on the inhabitants of the town, who seemed to be quite surprized, but nevertheless, as soon as they could get together, fought stoutly. They had some fire-arms, but made very little use of them, as they came directly to close fighting with their spears, lances and sabres. Many of the invaders were mounted on small horses, and both parties fought for about half an hour with the fiercest animosity, exerting much more courage and perseverance than I had ever before been witness to amongst them. The women and children of the town clustered together to the water's edge, running shrieking up and down with terror, waiting the event of the combat, till their party gave way, and took to the water, to endeavour to swim over to the Barbary side. They were closely pursued even into the river by the victors, who, though they came for the purpose of *getting slaves*, gave no quarter, their cruelty even prevailing over their avarice. They made no prisoners, but put all to the sword without mercy. Horrible indeed was the carnage of the vanquished on this occasion, and as we were within 200 or 300 yards of them, their cries and shrieks affected us extremely. We had got up our anchor

at

at the beginning of the fray, and now stood close in to the spot,
where the victors having followed the vanquished into the
water, were continually dragging out and murdering those
whom, by reason of their wounds, they easily overtook. The
very children, whom they took in great numbers, did not escape the massacre. Enraged at their barbarity, we fired our
guns, loaded with grape shot, and a volley of small arms
among them, which effectually checked their ardour, and
obliged them to retire to a distance from the shore; from whence
a few round cannon shot soon removed them into the woods.
The whole river was black over with the heads of the fugitives,
who were swimming for their lives. These poor wretches,
fearing us as much as their conquerors, dived when we fired,
and cried most lamentably for mercy. Having now effectually
favoured their retreat, we stood backwards and forwards, and
took up several that were wounded and tired. All whose
wounds had disabled them from swimming, were either butch-
ered or drowned before we got up to them. *With a justice and
generosity never, I believe, before heard of among slavers*, we gave
those their liberty whom we had taken up, setting them on
shore on the Barbary side, among the poor residue of their
companions, who had survived the slaughter of the morning.

On these undeniable facts concerning the mode of *procuring*
slaves at the first outset of the traffic, let the reader make his
own comments. They may be short; for he will have many
to make, ere the curtain is dropped over the melancholy picture
of Negro servitude.

As the Slave-coast, for reasons before mentioned, is not
over-burthened with native inhabitants; the slaves thus right-
eously procured, are brought from the Inland Country, frequently for the distance of 1000 or 1200 miles. The method of conveying them down to the coast, or to the ships, as
described by the Abbé Raynal (Hist. East and West Ind. iv.
12. Edinb. Ed.) is as follows. "Slave merchants are united
by mutual confederacy, and forming a species of caravans,
in 200 or 300 leagues they conduct several files of 30 or 40
slaves, all laden with water and corn, which are necessary to
their subsistence in those thirsty deserts through which they are
to pass. The method of securing them, without much in-
commoding their march, is ingeniously devised. A fork of
wood, from eight to nine feet long, is put round the neck of
each slave. A pin of iron, rivetted, secures the fork in such a
manner, that the head cannot disengage itself. The handle
of the fork, the wood of which is very heavy, falls before,
and so embarrasses the person who is tied to it, that though he
has

has his arms and legs free, he can neither walk, nor lift up the fork. When they get ready for their march, they range the slaves on the same line, and support and tie the extremity of each fork on the shoulder of the foremost slave, and proceed in this manner from one to another up to the first, the extremity of whose fork is carried by one of the guides. When these traders want sleep, they tie the arms of every slave to the tail of the fork which he carries. In this condition he can neither run a-way, nor make any attempt to regain his liberty. Thus far the Abbè Raynal's account.

The slaves thus brought down to the ships are examined, male and female, stark naked, by the surgeons of the vessels. Those who are picked out for sale, are immediately branded on the breast (with a red hot iron which lies ready in a fire for the pur-pose) with the arms and names of the Company, or Owners, who are the purchasers. This humane piece of caution being performed, the slaves are thrust by hundreds, males and females, promiscuously, into as small a place in the ship as the ingenuity of the owners can contrive to stow them in:

Immured

Within the scanty breadth of calculated inches.

To say nothing of the indecency of this practice, or of the unre-strained commerce of the sailors with the female slaves during the voyage, circumstances which are like the small dust in the balance of iniquity, the misery of a situation so extremely confined, the pe-stilential vapours they inhale, the badness of the provisions on which they are fed, the small quantity allowed them, and the tortures of a sultry climate, are frequently so great, that many slaves have been known to starve themselves to death on the voy-age; others, when brought upon deck for fresh air, have sprung over-board, to meet death in the waves; or have otherwise put an end to an existence so miserable, as to make a deliverance from it the greatest blessing they are capable of receiving. "O-thers, in a fit of despair, have attempted to rise, and regain their liberty. But here what a scene of barbarity has constantly en-sued. Some of them have been instantly killed on the spot: some have been taken from the hold, have been bruised and mutilated in the most barbarous and shocking manner, and have been returned bleeding to their companions, as a sad example of resistance: while others, tied to the ropes of the ship, and mangled alternately with the whip and the knife, have been left in that horrid situation till they have expired." Clarkson. 130

A confirmation of this account of Mr. Clarkson's, is a case mentioned in *Astley's* collection of Voyages by *John Atkins*, Sur-geon, on board Admiral *Ogle's* squadron, " of one *Harding*, mas-

ter

ter of a veffel, in which feveral of the men flaves, and a woman flave had attempted to rife, in order to recover their liberty: fome of whom the mafter, of his own authority, fentenced to cruel death; making them firft eat the heart and liver of one of thofe he killed. The woman he hoifted by the thumbs, whipt and flafhed with knifes before the other flaves till fhe died."

Benezet, who quotes this fact from Aftley's Voyages, adduces it as a parallel to another Inftance which he gives of the fame kind, from the account of a mafter of a Slave veffel on his arrival at Barbadoes.

He relates it from a perfon of undoubted credit who heard it from the captain's own mouth. Upon an enquiry what had been the fuccefs of his voyage, he anfwered, That he found it a difficult matter to fet the Negroes a fighting with each other, in order to procure the number he wanted: but that when he had obtained this end, and had got his veffel filled with flaves, a new difficulty arofe from their refufal to take food: thofe defperate creatures choofing to die with hunger, rather than be carried from their native country. Upon a farther enquiry by what means he had prevailed upon them, to forego this defperate refolution, he anfwered, " That he obliged all the negroes to come upon deck, where they perfifted in their refolution of not taking food; he caufed his failors to lay hold upon one of the moft obftinate, and chopt the poor creature into fmall pieces, forcing fome of the others to eat a part of the mangled body; withal fwearing to the furvivors that he would ufe them all one after another in the fame manner if they did not confent to eat." "This horrid execution he applauded as a good act, it having had the defired effect in bringing them to take food. Benezet's Caution, &c. Page 26.

Should any tempeftuous weather arife during the voyage, or fhould provifions run fhort in any degree, the requifite number of flaves are thrown overboard without any fcruple, to lighten the cargo, or leffen the number of mouths. Nay, within thefe few years, no lefs than 132 flaves were thrown over-board within two or three days from one fhip, not becaufe the weather required it, or provifions were fcanty, but becaufe the captain had a defire to defraud the underwriters, in favour of the fhip owners. The circumftance, tho' not very fingular perhaps, is fo much out of the way of any tranfaction which does not happen with a Slave-trader, that the narrative is worth tranfcribing.

In March 1783, the following Circumftances came out in evidence on a Cafe of Infurance, tried in the Court of King's Bench, Weftminfter. On the 6th of September, 1781, the fhip
Zong

Zong or Zurg, Luke Collingwood, mafter, failed from the Ifland of St. Thomas for Jamaica, with about 440 negroes, and 17 white perfons on board. On the 27th of November following fhe fell in with the place of her deftination; but the maf- ter, either thro' ignorance or defign, ran the fhip to *leeward,* alledging that he miftook it for Hifpaniola. About this time (as is ufual in flave fhips) a violent ficknefs and mortality raged on board; fo that from the time of her leaving Africa, to the 29th of November, not lefs than 60 flaves and 7 white perfons died, and a great number of the remaining flaves were fick of the fame diftemper. The quantity of mouths, therefore, inftead of being encreafed, and thereby caufing a fcarcity, were confider- ably leffened.

Collingwood, however, now difcovered or pretended to dif- cover, that their ftock of frefh water was reduced to 200 gallons: therefore there was no *prefent* want of water: they were not yet put to fhort allowance: there was great probability moreover that it would rain in a few days, as indeed it did, and at all events they might have made an enemy's port in 24 hours. The plea of neceffity, therefore, could not be the true reafon of the fubfequent murder. Collingwood calling together a few of the officers, told them, "That if the flaves died a natural death, it would be to the lofs of the owners, but if they were thrown a- live into the fea, the lofs would be the underwriters." To this propofal the chief mate (who was an evidence in the caufe) at firft objected, obferving that there was no prefent want of wa- ter, and therefore no excufe for fuch a meafure. He and the reft of the crew were, however, foon perfuaded, and the fame evening the mafter felected 132 flaves, all of whom were fick and weak, and or dered them to be thrown into the fea. On the 29th of November, 54 innocent and unhappy perfons were thrown over-board alive, and on the following day 42 more, making 96 out of the 132. On the firft of December, and for a day or two following, there fell a plentiful *rain,* which enabled them to collect *fix cafks of water,* and took away the fole argument for putting to death the negroes, viz. the plea of wanting water. The fate of the unfortunate victims was, however, pre determined, *and even after the rain* 26 *negroes were thrown over-board* with their hands fettered or bound, and in the fight of feveral others who were brought upon the deck for the fame purpofe, ten of whom, to avoid the unneceffary cruelty of having their hands confined, jumped over-board and were alfo drowned. The fhip, after all, brought into port 480 gallons of water. The *humane* owners affected to cenfure the *imprudence* of the murderer. The under- writers hefitating to make good the infurance, this action en- fued.

fued.—The above account is extracted chiefly in the words of Dr. Gregory * (Essays, 307) with an additional circumstance or two from Mr. Ramsay.

This Anecdote (shocking as it is, says Dr. Gregory) is not without a parallel, for not many years ago a vessel from Africa, freighted with negro slaves, was run on shore in the Island of Jamaica. The master and crew saved themselves in the boat, and thro' I know not what unnecessary fears for their own safety, knocked the negroes on the head as they swam on sho re.(ibid.)

From the loading of the vessels at the African coast, to the completion of the voyage, there is an average dimuntion of the original number of slaves, one fifth. The routine of occurrences to which the remaining four-fifths are subject, I shall relate in the words of Mr. Clarkson, who having attended very particularly to the subject, and having had frequent opportunities of information, from gentlemen long resident in the British plantations, is more competent to state the facts, and better able to supply the language suitable to the occasion, than I can pretend to be.

When the ship arrives at its destined port, they are again exposed to sale. Here they are again subjected to the inspection of other brutal *receivers*, who examine and treat them with an inhumanity at which even Avarice would blush. To this mortifying circumstance is added another—that they are picked out as the purchaser pleases, without any consideration whether the wife is separated from her husband, or the mother from her son : and if these cruel instances of separation should happen ; if relations, when they find themselves about to be parted, should cling together; or if filial, conjugal, or parental affection should detain them but a moment longer in each others arms than these *second receivers* should think fit, the lash instantly severs them from their embraces.

When the wretched Africans are conveyed to the plantations, they are considered as *beasts of labour*, and are put to their respective work. Having led in their own country a life of indolence and ease, where the earth brings forth spontaneously the comforts of life, and spares frequently the toil and trouble of cultivation, they can hardly be expected to endure the drudgeries of servitude. Calculations are accordingly made upon their lives. It is conjectured that if three in four survive what is called the *seasoning*, the bargain is highly favourable. This seasoning is said to expire when the two first years of their servitude is completed. It is the time which an African must take to
be

* I forgot to enumerate among the Writers against the Slave-trade, Dr. Gregory's excellent Essay on this Subject : but it deserved not to be omitted.

be fo accuftomed to the colony, as to be able to endure the common labour of a plantation, and to be put in the *gang*. At this period they are confidered as real and fubftantial fupplies. From this period therefore we fhall defcribe their fituation. They are fummoned at five in the morning to begin their work. The work may be divided into two kinds, the culture of the fields, and the collection of grafs for the cattle. The laft is the moft laborious and intolerable employment; as the grafs can only be collected blade by blade, and is to be fetched frequently twice a day, at a confiderable diftance from the plantation. In thefe two occupations they are jointly taken up, with no other intermiffion than that of taking their fubfiftence twice, till nine at night. They then feparate for their refpective huts, when they gather fticks, prepare their fupper, and attend their families. This employs them till midnight, when they go to reft. Such is their daily way of life for rather more than half the year. They are 16 hours, including two intervals at meals, in the fervice of their mafters—they are employed three hours afterwards in their own neceffary concerns—five only remain for fleep, and the day is finifhed.

During the remaining portion of the year, or the time of crop, the nature, as well as the time of their employment, is confiderably changed. The whole gang is generally divided into two or three bodies. One of thefe, *befides the ordinary labour of the day*, is kept in turn at the mills, which are conftantly going during the whole of the night. This is a dreadful encroachment upon their time of reft, which was before too fhort to permit them perfectly to refrefh their wearied limbs, and actually reduces their fleep, as long as this feafon lafts, to about three hours and a half each night, upon a moderate computation.— Thofe who can keep their eyes open during their nightly labour, and are willing to refift the drowfinefs that is continually coming upon them, are prefently worn out; while fome of thofe who are overcome, and who feed the mill between afleep and awake, fuffer for thus obeying the calls of nature, by the lofs of a limb; a hand or arm being frequently ground off. In this manner they go on, with little or no refpite from their work, till the crop feafon is over, when the year (from the time of our firft defcription) is completed.

To fupport a life of fuch unparalleled drudgery, we fhould at leaft expect to find that they were comfortably cloathed, and plentifully fed. But, fad reverfe! they have fcarcely a covering againft the inclemency of the night. Their provifions are frequently bad, and are always dealt out to them with fuch a

fparing

fparing hand, that the means of a bare livelihood are not placed
within the reach of four out of five of thofe unhappy people.

It is a fact that many of the diforders of flaves are contracted
from eating the vegetables which their little fpots produce, before they are ripe: a clear indication that the calls of hunger
are fo prefling, as not to fuffer them to wait till they can really
enjoy them. Neitherwill this ftatement be deemed in the flighteft
degree a deviation from the literal truth in favour of the flaves,
when the reader is informed of what is an undeniable fact, name-
ly, that a flave's *annual* allowance from his mafter, for provifions, cloathing, medicines when fick, &c. is limited upon an
average to THIRTY SHILLINGS!

This fituation of the want of the common neceffaries of life,
added to that of hard and continual labour, muft be fufficiently
painful of itfelf. How then muft the pain be fharpened, if it
be accompanied with feverity? If an unfortunate flave does
not come into the field exactly at the appointed time; if, droop-
ing with ficknefs or fatigue, he appears to work unwillingly;
or if the bundle of grafs he has been collecting appears too fmall
in the eye of the Overfeer, he is equally fure of experiencing
the whip.—This inftrument erafes the fkin, and cuts out fmall
portions of the flefh at almoft every ftroke; and is fo frequently
applied, that the fmack of it is all day long in the ears of thofe
who are in the vicinity of the plantations. This feverity of
mafters or managers to their flaves, which is confidered only as
common difcipline, is attended with bad effects. It enables
them to behold inftances of cruelty without commiferation, and
to be guilty of them without remorfe. Hence thofe many acts
of deliberate mutilation, that have taken place on the flighteft
occafions: hence thofe many inftances of inferior, but fhocking
barbarity, which have taken place without any occafion at all.
The very *flitting of ears* has been confidered as an operation fo
perfectly devoid of pain, as to have been performed for no other
reafon than that for which a brand is fet upon cattle, as a *mark
of property*.

But this is not the only effect which this feverity produces,
for while it hardens their hearts, and makes them infenfible of
the mifery of their fellow-creatures, it begets a turn for wanton
cruelty. As a proof of this, we fhall only mention one among
the many inftances that occur, where ingenuity has been exerted
in inventing inftruments of torture. "An iron coffin, with
holes in it, was kept by a certain colonift, as an auxiliary
to the lafh. In this the poor victim of the mafter's refentment
was inclofed, and placed fufficiently near a fire to occafion extreme pain, and confequently fhrieks and groans, until the re-
venge

venge of the mafter was fatiated, without any other inconvenience on his part, than a temporary fufpenfion of the flave's labour. Had he been flogged to death, or his limbs mutilated,
the intereft of the brutal tyrant would have fuffered a more ir-
reparable lofs." (Clarkfon's Effay, 138 et fec.)

"Gentlemen who have refided in the Ifland of Jamaica during three or four years of the laft war, and who out of curiofity
have frequented the markets where thofe unhappy people weekly
refort, have remarked that they have not been able to turn their
eyes on any group of them whatever, but they have beholden
the inhuman marks of paffion, defpotifm and caprice, in the
flitting of ears, eyes beaten out, and limbs broken." Clarkfon. 151.

The account given in the very accurate tract of Mr. Wefley,
of the mode of treatment of the negroes on their landing at the
plantations; of the labour they are enjoined; of the manner
wherein they are fed, and the punifhment they receive, perfectly
tallies with the preceding defcription of Mr. Clarkfon. But as
fome facts are mentioned by the former, not noticed by the latter, I fhall make an extract from Mr. Wefley's publication.
Having mentioned their general treatment, he proceeds, p. 26.
8. "As to the punifhments inflicted on them," fays Sir Hans
Sloane, "they frequently geld them, or chop off half a foot.
After they are whipt till they are raw all over, fome put pepper
and falt upon them; fome drop melted wax upon their fkin;
others cut off their ears, and conftrain them to broil and eat
them. For rebellion (that is afferting their native liberty,
which they have as much a right to as the air they breathe) they
fasten them down to the ground with crooked fticks on every
limb, and then applying fire by degrees to the feet and hands,
they burn them gradually upwards to the head."

9. But will not the laws, made in the plantations, prevent
and redrefs all cruelty and oppreffion? We will take but a few
of thefe Laws, as a fpecimen, and then let every man judge.

In order to rivet the chain of Slavery, the law of Virginia
ordains, "That no Slave fhall be fet free upon any pretence
whatever, except for fome meritorious fervices, to be adjudged
and allowed by the Governor and Council. And that where
any flave fhall be fet free by his owner, otherwife than is herein
directed, the Church-Wardens, of the Parifh wherein fuch
negro fhall refide for the fpace of one month, are hereby autho-
rifed and required *to take up and fell the faid negro by public outcry.*"

Will not thefe law-givers take effectual care to prevent cruelty
and oppreffion?

The law of Jamaica ordains, "Every flave that fhall run

C   away,

away, and be absent from his master 12 months, shall be deemed
rebellious. And by another law, 50l. are allowed to th se who
shall kill or bring in alive a *rebellious* slave. So their law treats
these poor men, with as little ceremony and consideration as if
they were merely brute beasts! But the innocent blood which
is shed in consequence of such a detestable law, must call for
vengeance on the murderous abettors and actors of such deliberate wickedness.

But the law of *Barbadoes* exceeds even this. "If any negro
under punishment by his master, or his order, for running away,
or any other crime or misdemeanor, *shall suffer in life or member,
no person whatever shall be liable to any fine therefore.* But if any man
of *wantonness*, or *bloody-mindedness*, or *cruel intention*, wilfully kill
a negro of his own (now observe the severe punishment!) he
shall pay into the public treasury 15l. sterling! and not be liable
to any other punishment, or forfeiture for the same!" Act the
39th.

Nearly allied to this is the law of Virginia. "After procla-
mation is issued against slaves that run away, it is lawful for any
person, whatever, to kill and destroy such slaves, *by such ways
and means as he shall think fit.*"

We have seen already some of the ways and means, which
have been *thought fit* on such occasions;--and many more might
be mentioned. *One gentleman, when I was abroad, thought fit to
roast his slave alive!* But if the most natural act of running
away from intolerable tyranny, deserves such relentless severity,
what punishment have these *law-makers* to expect hereafter, on
account of their own enormous offences!

This is the plain unaggravated matter of fact. Such is the
manner wherein our African slaves are procured: such the manner wherein they are removed from their native land, and wherein they are treated in our plantations. Thus far the Rev. Mr.
Westley: chiefly from Benezet.

That negroes, in our plantations, are thus treated, some
have affected to disbelieve or deny. It will be proper, therefore,
to corroborate these accounts, by passages from other writers of
credit on this part of the History of Negro Servitude.

The following extract of a letter from a gentleman in Mary-
land to his friend in London, I give on the authority of Mr.
Grenville Sharp.

"The punishments of the poor negroes and convicts, are
beyond all conception: being entirely subject to the will of their
savage and brutal masters, they are often punished for not doing
more than strength and nature will admit of, and sometimes because they can't, on every occasion, fall in with their wanton
and

and capricious humours. One common punishment is to flea their backs with cow-hides, or other instruments of barbarity, and then pour on hot rum, superinduced with brine or pickle, rubbed in with a corn husk in the scorching heat of the sun." (From the 2d. Appendix to Sharp's Limitation of Slavery.)

Sir Hans Sloan, in his history of Jamaica, speaks " of the horrid executions frequently made there upon discovery of the Plots laid by the Blacks for the recovery of their Liberty: of some they break the bones whilst alive, upon a wheel; others they burn or rather roast to death; others they starve to death with a loaf hanging before their mouths." The Rev. Mr. Ramsay, who speaks from twenty years experience and fourteen years particular attention to the subject, after giving an account of the Labour of the negroes in the Sugar plantations, in no respect materially different from the preceding Extract from Mr. Clarkson's Essay, proceeds. (Essay p. 74,) " The work here mentioned is considered as the field duty of Slaves, that may be insisted on without reproach to the manager of unusual severity, and which the white and black Overseers stand over them to see executed; the transgression against which is quickly followed by the smart of the cart whip. This instrument, in the hands of a skilful driver, cuts out flakes of skin and flesh with every Stroke, and the wretch in this mangled condition is turned out to work in dry or wet weather, which last now and then brings on the cramp, and ends his slavery and his sufferings together."

" The ordinary punishment for slaves (page 85) for the common crimes of neglect, absence from work, eating the sugar cane, theft, are cart whipping, beating with a stick, sometimes to the breaking of bones, the chain, an iron crook about the neck, a large iron pudding, or ring about the ancle, and confinement in the dungeon. There have been instances of flitting of ears, breaking of limbs so as to make amputation necessary, beating out of eyes, and castration; but they seldom happen, especially of late years, and *tho' they bring no lasting disgrace on the perpetrator*, have for some time past been generally mentioned with Indignation. It is *yet* true, that the unfeeling application of the ordinary punishment, ruins the constitution, and shortens the life of many a poor wretch!

In a certain Colony, no less than two *Chief Judges* within these thirty Years have been celebrated for cutting off or mashing (so as to make amputation necessary) the limbs of their slaves. In one case a Surgeon was called in to operate—he answered, he was not obliged to be the instrument of another man's cruelty. His honour had it then performed by a Cooper's Adze, and the wretch was left to bleed to death without attention or dressing.

When

When he became convulfed in the agonies of death the furgeon was again haftily fent for, and came in time to pronounce him dead. People ftared at the recital, but made no enquiry for blood. In the other cafe the limb was mafhed with a fledge hammer, and then it was amputated by a Surgeon, and the maimed wretch lived fome Years." (ibid. note p. 86.)

This account of Mr. Ramfay's, being difcredited by the anonymous defenders of Slavery, Capt. James Smith, to whom a Clergyman had lent Mr. Ramfay's Effay, voluntarily offered his corroborating Teftimony. From his Letter I have made the following extract.

" The ill treatment of flaves is too well known and too univerfal to be denied. I do affirm I have feen the moft cruel treatment made ufe of at feveral of the Weft India Iflands, particularly at Antigua. While ferving on that ftation ten years ago, I vifited feveral of the Plantations there. In confequence of meeting with an old School-fellow, who managed an eftate on that ifland, I was introduced to many of that defcription ; and too often has my heart ached to fee the cruel punifhments for trifling caufes inflicted by the Manager, with fuch unconcern as not to break in upon his jocularity. When I have interfered, I have been afked, " Do you not punifh on board Ships"? My anfwer was, " Yes, no doubt ; but not in this cruel way." A poor negro is laid ftretched flat on his face on the ground, at his peril to move an inch till the punifhment is over; that is inflicted with a whip, whofe thong at the thickeft part was the fize of a man's thumb, and tapering longer than a coachman's whip. At every ftroke a piece was taken out by the particular jerk of the whip, which the Manager (fometimes his wife) takes care to direct. This I have often feen, for not getting a fufficient quantity of grafs for the Manager, (for I well know more goes to his fhare than his mafter's) and many fuch trifling things." (Capt. James Smith's letter to the Rev. Mr. Hill, p. 12. 13.)

" The hours of labour (fays Dr. Gregory, Effays 308) are 16, and at the very leaft 14 out of the 24; and the exertions required are frequently more than their natural ftrength and conftitution will bear. A perfon of veracity affured me, that he has feen in one of our Weft India Iflands, a flender female with a child at her back, compelled to carry up a high ladder 17 Briftol bricks, during the whole of a fummer's day. When her ftrength was exhaufted fhe fat down, and in the bitternefs of her foul burft into a flood of tears; but fo little of humanity exifted in the breaft of her tafk-mafter, that he immediately roufed her to a renewal of her labour, by a fevere flagellation."

" The

" The common inftrument to keep them to their work is a
whip like the *Ruffian knout*, which flays off the fkin wherever it
is applied; the moft merciful is a *goad*, like that which is ufed
to oxen, but fomewhat longer; and let it be remembered, that
the ufe of thefe inftruments is frequently at the *difcretion* of a
tranfport; or fome of the moft drunken and abandoned domef-
tics of a Planter!" (ibid 309)

" If, under thefe complicated injuries, an effort is made to
recover the natural rights of man; on difcovery, the fentence
is of a piece with the cruelty which occafioned the crime. The
trials are very fummary; the evidence required very flight;
the Judges too often ignorant; the jury (*the Mafters*) preju-
diced; fo that I doubt not but innocence too often fuffers.
Gibbetting alive is always the punifhment for this, as well as for
all other capital offences. I knew a gentleman who had feen
in Antigua fome of thefe wretches exift on the gibbet to the
ninth day, with a loaf of bread hung at the end of the gibbet,
to enhance the torture."

" But it is not for real crimes only, that the unhappy fub-
jects of thefe pages are doomed to fuffer. I believe the following is a fact, which is generally allowed. As the govern-
ment always pays the full price for any negro, who fuffers
death upon conviction of felony; when an unprincipled planter has *an old negro*, who is paft his labour, and confequently
(as they term it) a dead weight upon the plantation, the
planter takes care to ftarve him, till the negro is reduced by
hunger to a ftate of defperation; fome provifion is then laid
in his way, in order to tempt him to fteal; which, if he does,
he is dragged to juftice, he is executed, and the deliberate
murderer pockets the wages of blood and cruelty." (ibid 310.)

" Thefe facts, fays Dr. Gregory, which I have adduced,
I have taken on the beft authority. I have found them corro-.
borated by many impartial teftimonies; and from the reafon
of things, and the nature of flavery, there is great reafon to
believe, that this ftate of the cafe is not exaggerated." (ibid
313.)

That there will be fome difference in the treatment of flaves,
according to the different tempers and degrees of knowledge
of the Britifh Planters or Managers, there is no doubt; but if
the reader wifhes for *farther* authorities to prove, that the *general* ftate of the negroes in the Britifh plantations, is fuch as
I have here reprefented it, I refer him to the corroborative teftimony of the Abbè Raynal, Hift. philofophique, &c. v. 4
p. 5 to 7.

Dean Tucker's Reflections on the Difputes between Great
Britain

Britain and Ireland, p. 8 17.   Account of the European Set-
tlements in America (attributed to Burke) v. 2. p. 120—127.

To this account, other circumstances of cruelty and extreme indecency might easily be added, such as I myself have
heard from the relation of eye witnesses, whose character will
not permit that I should suspect them of falshood; but I spare
the Reader from these shocking scenes; and I tempt him not to
the perusal of transactions which are related with hesitancy, and
heard with a blush, by every man who is not in some measure
concerned in their commission.

How much has it been the fashion for Englishmen to vaunt
of their own love of freedom, and to exclaim against the cruel-
ties of the Spaniards in South America! The facts just stated,
however, will shew how little we value the cause of freedom,
where our own emancipation is not concerned. And with
how little knowledge, and how much injustice we exclaim
against *Spanish* cruelty, the following account of the Spanish
regulations, respecting their slaves, will fully evince.

As soon as a Slave is landed, his name, price, &c. are re-
gistered in a public register, and the Master is obliged, by law,
to allow him one working day in every week to himself, be-
sides Sunday.   So that if the slave chooses to work for his master on that day, he receives the wages of a freeman for it;
and whatever he gains by his labour on that day, is so secured
to him by law, that his master cannot deprive him of it.   As
soon as the slave is able to purchase another working day, the
master is obliged to sell it him, at a proportionable price; viz.
one fifth part of his original cost; and so likewise the remaining four days at the same rate, as soon as the slave is able to
redeem them, after which he is absolutely free.   This is such
an encouragement to industry, that even the most indolent are
tempted to exert themselves.   Men, who have thus worked
out their freedom, are enured to the labour of the country, and
are certainly the most useful subjects, that a colony can ac-
quire.   (Sharp's Limit of Slavery, 55.)

In the same spirit are framed the French regulations of the
Code Noir; while, to the utter disgrace of Englishmen, they
not only procure slaves for themselves and others, but they
leave them exposed to the wanton barbarity of every low bred
despot.

The average import of slaves into the European colonies may
be 100,000.   But these are only two-thirds of the import pre-
vious to the seasoning; for one third dies in the seasoning;
therefore the actual import into the European colonies, is, at
this rate, 150,000.   But this latter number is only four-fifths
of

of the cargo when firſt laden ; for one fifth at leaſt dies in the paſſage; therefore the cargo, when firſt laden, was 180,000 men. Moreover it has been obſerved before, and proof has been offered fully ſufficient to eſtabliſh the faƐt, that for *one* man aƐtually ſent down to the coaſt, at the very leaſt *ten* were ſlaughtered. Hence *one million eight hundred thouſand* people are annually murdered at the inſtigation of Europeans, to furniſh them with an annual ſupply of 100,000 poor wretches to do that work, which, after all, they might, confiſtently with their health, perform themſelves !

That 100,000 is the average annual confumption, is generally allowed ; and this computation is confirmed by the following ſtatement of the Abbé Raynal. (Hiſt. Ind. Book 11) In 1768 there were exported out of Africa 104000 ſlaves. The Engliſh have exported 53,100 for their iſlands ; their Coloniſts on the North continent carried away 6300; the French 23,500 ; the Dutch 11,300 ; the Portugueſe 8,700 ; and the Danes 1200. This account alfo tallies with the concluſions deducible from the following faƐt, fince publiſhed by authority. In 96 years, ending in 1774, 800,000 ſlaves had been imported into the French part of St. Domingo, of which there remained only 290,000 in 1774. Of this laſt number only 140,000 were Creoles, or natives of the iſland ; i. e. of 650,000 ſlaves, the whole poſterity was 140,000. (Confiderations fur la Colonie de Dominique.)— Compare this with the faƐt of the duplication of inhabitants throughout the American continent in 25 years, and allow for emigrants into the bargain !—Let it alfo be confidered, that the French ſlaves are incomparably better treated than the Engliſh, in confequence of the humane regulations of the Code Noir.

The Abbé Raynal computes, that at the time of his writing, nine millions of ſlaves had been confumed by the Europeans. Add one million at leaſt fince, for it is about 10 years ago. Recolleƈting then, that for one ſlave procured, ten at leaſt are ſlaughtered ; that a fifth die in the paſſage, and a third in the feafoning ; and the unexaggerated computation will turn out, that the infernal voracity of European avarice has been glutted with the MURDER of ONE HUNDRED and EIGHTY MILLIONS of our FELLOW-CREATURES ! Good God, cries the aſtoniſhed Reader, for what purpoſe ?———*That the Gentlefolk of Europe, (my friend) may drink Sugar to their Tea ! !*

Such is the extent of the Charity which now ſolicits the Aſfiſtance of the Benevolent. That if the wifdom and humanity of the Legiſlature cannot interfere fo far as to exterminate a traffic fo replete with iniquity, fome bounds at leaſt may be ſet to the wantonnefs of cruelty, and the tyranny of avarice. That

if

if the demands of commerce require that Negroes fhall be enflaved becaufe they are black, and doomed to perpetual labour
becaufe their native climate is warm, fome line fhall be drawn,
beyond which oppreffion fhall not be exerted, and fome fmall
alleviation fupplied to miferies, which, though called on by
Compaffion, by Juftice, and Religion, we have nót the courage
to end.

An application to Parliament will be attended with much trouble, and cannot effectually be profecuted without much expence.
Hitherto the Subfcriptions for this humane purpofe, have been
confined to individuals of the refpectable fet of QUAKERS. But
why fhould the caufe of humanity be fupported by any particular defcription of the human race?

But if *particular claffes* of individuals may with fo much propriety intereft themfelves on an occafion fo praife-worthy, are
there none but the *Quakers*, who may reafonably be expected to
ftand forth the advocates of the injured and oppreffed? Whatever may be the peculiar opinions of the various denominations
of *Chriftians*, furely there can be no difference in opinion in a cafe
fo obvious. Even warmth may be forgiven, if it mingle with the
mildnefs of Chriftianity, on the recollection of circumftances
of fuch enormous wickednefs, when even our Lord himfelf
fpeaks with extreme indignation of thofe who offend againft the
firft Law of Benevolence, Charity, or Love. " Wo unto you,
Scribes and Pharifees, hypocrites; ye pay tithe of mint, anife,
and cummin, and neglect the *weightier matters of the Law,
Judgment, and* MERCY. Thefe things ought ye to have done,
and not to have left the other undone. Ye ferpents, ye genera-
tion of vipers, how can ye efcape the Damnation of Hell!"

May I prefume to mention to the Gentlemen of the *Eftablifhment*, whofe lives and converfations do fo much honour to the
pro effional character in this town and neighbourhood, and many
of whom even now occur to my recollection, who are poffeffed
of abilities and eloquence far beyond the common portion which
their fellow-labourers in the vineyard at large enjoy—altho' the
poft of honour, in this moft honourable conflict with Tyrany
and Cruelty, has been feized by fectaries, that it would not be
inconfiftent with their own private feelings, with their private
character, with their public character, with their profeffional
duty, to join with their Fellow Chriftians in a point wherein
no Chriftians *can* differ, and affift, to their utmoft, endeavours
fo laudably exerted. The prefent Bifhop of Chefter has already
fet the example of preaching at a public charity, (for fuch *in
fact* is the Society for the Propagation of the Gofpel) a Charity
Sermon, in favour of fome alleviation to Negro Servitude: he

has

has enforced it, from the conduct and opinion of those whom *Englishmen* ought deeply to blush that they have not preceded, the *French* and the *Spanish*. What if the Clergy of Manchester were to recommend to their respective Congregations, in an expres Discourse, to contribute their Mite toward the subscription for the Parliamentary application? Surely such liberality of sentiment and conduct would reflect honour upon the sacred character, and shew that diversity in matters of mere opinion, will never prevent their adopting uniformity in practical benevolence.

To the Society of *Quakers* in this town, I apprehend it will be unnecessary to say much, to incite them to promote what the sect have almost *universally* adopted, with a zeal, a perseverance, an attention, a liberality to which no praise can be equal.— The *Friends* in Manchester will certainly not remain singular in a matter so honourable to themselves and their profession. A-mong the *Presbyterians* in America, the Question relating to Universal Manumission was negatived by ONE only. Since then, other facts have come to light, other enormities have been observed, and the experiment of Manumission extensively tried, has, *even lucratively,* answered. Why should not the inhabitants of Manchester, the Teachers in particular of this persuasion, second the exertions of the respectable Minority abroad, and complete, as far as the present application can extend, what was left undone by their American brethren? I am not solicitous to distinguish, among the numerous and opulent Dissenters in Manchester, who rank under the denomination of *Presbyterians*, those of the Arian from those of the Calvinistic persuasion. For what has such a distinction to do in the present case? This is not the cause of Arianism or of Calvinism—it is the cause of Humanity, of Christianity.

But I apply particularly to the Methodists: to those who must have read, or have heard at least, of the very excellent Tract of that very excellent man the Rev. John Westley. They are a disgrace to their Character, they are a disgrace to their Leader, if this Pamphlet has not made a forcible impression on their minds. " To turn the hearts of the Disobedient to the Wisdom of the Just," has certainly been the earnest endeavour of the chief promoters of methodism, whatever may have been the characters of some of their followers, or whatever may have been the propriety or impropriety of the means used towards this great end. My friends, for this end you are again called upon: I call upon the Preachers among you to second the endeavours of their great Master. This is the cause of Benevolence and Religion: it is therefore the cause of Methodism. Do yourselves honour, and haste to come forth the foremost in this business. The omission will disgrace you.

D   Whatever

Whatever may be the religious perfuafion of the Reader, upon the principles of his own fect, he may fairly be addreffed. He that is not with us, is againft us. As Englifhmen, the blood of the murdered African is upon us, and upon our children, and in fome day of retribution he will feel it, who will not affift to wafh off the ftain.

But why thefe addreffes to the inhabitants of Manchefter in their religious characters only? There is not a man of common honefty, of any, or of no religion, who, on due confideration, can deny that this fhocking traffic is downright rebellion againft the plaineft principles of common honefty. I appeal therefore to every man who affumes this character, not merely in behalf of the caufe, but in behalf of his own confiftency. And I hope the inhabitants of Manchefter, who have purchafed and enjoyed fuch public reputation for their fpirited exertions againft political oppreffion, will not want fpirit in fuch a caufe as this, merely becaufe their peculiar intereft is not concerned. I appeal to themfelves what honour they have it now in their power to gain, by a marked, a public interference in a caufe of fuch magnitude, and fo reputable; and I hope an Appeal on fuch a Subject will not be made in vain.

APPENDIX.

APPENDIX.

I Did not think it worth while to infert in the body of this fe-
lection the arguments, or rather the excufes which flave-
dealers and flave-holders alledge in reply to the charges adduced
againft them. A fhort ftatement, however, of thefe excufes, and
the obvious repiies, may not be improper in a pamphlet which is
intended for general information. I fhall therefore ftate what I
have heard or perufed in favour of the African trade either in
converfation or in print; and this in the order of the preceding
hiftorical deduction of this traffic. As to the mode of procuring
flaves on the coaft. It is faid,

I. Whatever may have been the cafe, the flaves are now purchafed; and therefore it is the bufinefs of the feller, and not of
the purchafer, to take care that they are properly procured ori-
ginally.

Anfwer I. It is notorious that we ourfelves kidnap the negroes on every opportunity. 2. It is notorious that the flave
dealers, from whom we purchafe them, are kidnappers. 3. We
do ftill incite and encourage wars on the coaft, for the purpofe of
making flaves plentiful. 4. Before any man purchafes a flave,
who alledges the injuftice of the fale, it is the duty of the purchafer to take care that the labour of the perfon fold was properly forfeited, for there is, primâ facie, evidence againft this.

II. The Perfons fold, are fold by the authority of their prince,
and are in general convicts. Anf. 1. No prince has a right to
fell his fubject; nor has an Englifhman a right to encourage tyranny. 2. It is notorious that an extremely fmall portion are
convicts. 3. Of thofe who are, the majority are unjuftly condemned; and it is well known that capital crimes, which
induce the flavery, not only of the perfon guilty, but of his
whole family, are made very numerous by the African tyrants,
that their revenue may be increafed, by the fale of the perfons
condemned, 4. In the moft civilized European ftates, the
punifhments are too difproportionate and fevere: a fortiori,
they are likely to be fo in ftates fo imperfectly civilized. Hence
the obligation is very ftrong upon us, to take care that we are
not, from carelefsnefs or wilful negligence, the inftruments of
injuftice and oppreflion.

III. There

III. There is no cruelty in purchasing the negroes as flaves, becaufe they are univerfally fo in their own country.

Anfwer 1. If they are fo, fo much the worfe: It is our duty to extend political freedom, and not flavery. 2. They are not flaves to their prince in the fame fenfe as they become fo to the purchafers. 3. The Africans are all extremely fond of their own country, and abhor extremely their Weft-Indian fervitude.

As to the mode of *treating* them on board fhip, and their *plantation punifhments*—it is faid,

IV. Such feverity is abfolutely neceffary, to prevent mutiny, and compel labour.

Anfwer 1. As far as the experiment has been tried, general mild treatment, with certain and fevere, but not brutally-cruel punifhments, have anfwered beft. Facts to this purpofe have been furnifhed by Mr. Ramfay and Captain Smith, and the French plantations are ftanding proofs of this. 2. Becaufe one act of cruelty and injuftice makes feveral others neceffary— the firft does not juftify the fubfequent ones. It is no juftification of my murderer, that I refufed to be robbed.

V. One may ufe a negro like a brute animal, for they are a different race of beings.

Anfwer 1. We treat no brute animals fo ill. 2. If we did, the treatment is too cruel to admit of juftification. 3. They are men; fufceptible of the fame cultivation with ourfelves. A white and a black do not produce a mule, but a being capable of continuing the fpecies; which is the very ftrongeft proof of famenefs of fpecies. The whitenefs of a white man decreafes in hot climates, and the blacknefs of the black man in cold ones. As to their capacity, let the Poems of Phillis Wheatley, and the Letters of Ignatius Sancho be perufed, and the queftion is decided. By the way; the mother of Ignatius Sancho was hurried on board a flave fhip, pregnant: on board the fhip Sancho was born: with difficulty he was kept alive: but his father receiving the common treatment of plantation negroes, thought fit to put an end to his own exiftence.

VI. It is denied that the treatment of the negroes is fuch as has been reprefented: it is moreover improbable that it fhould, for it is againft the planters' intereft.

Anfwer 1. The fact has been anonymoufly denied: I have proved it by fuch teftimonies as Benezet, Wefley, Grenville Sharp, Ramfay, Capt. Hill, Clarkfon, Dr. Gregory—to which may be added the concurrent belief of Raynal, Dean Tucker, Burke, &c. I forbear to quote the anonymous corroborators. No impartial man believes otherwife, than that the anonymous deniers of thefe notorious facts deny, for interefted

purpofes,

APPENDIX.

purpofes, what they know to be true. 2. Every body knows, that intereft will very often be facrificed to paffion. 3. In the Britifh plantations the cafe very generally is, that the perfon who in-flicts the cruel punifhments complained of, facrifices not his own, but his mafter's intereft, who is fpending the profits of the plantation in Great Britain; and who cannot afford that the flaves fhall not be worked to the utmoft of their ftrength. 4. The fact is, that the intereft of the Britifh planters is prodigioufly facrificed by the treatment in queftion. The French flaves are all well treated; *but the planters themfelves refide on their own plantations.*

VII. The planters have a right to the utmoft labour of the flaves, for they have paid for it. Anfwer 1. No bargain is fair, where there is not a *quid pro quo*; a mutual equivalent. But no equivalent can poffibly be received by the flave. 2. No man has a right to purchafe what he may know, if he pleafe, that the feller has no right to fell.

VIII. The iflands could not be cultivated without flaves; becaufe white men cannot bear labour in fo warm a climate, while blacks can; and becaufe even if the negroes were manumitted, no free negro will work as a day labourer; which is evinced by the indolence of the Caribs in St. Vincents, and the Marons in Jamaica. Anfwer 1. It is better that the iflands remained uncultivated to eternity, than that their cultivation fhould be encouraged at the price of fuch enormous, fuch extenfive villany. If thefe be juftifiable means of becoming rich, with what face can we put to death the man who fhoots another through the head for the purpofe of fecuring the contents of the dead man's pocket? 2. It is in all cafes impolitic to force colonization. 3. The whites can cultivate the iflands much better than the blacks. For thofe are capable of the greateft exertion, who have been perpetually accuftomed to exertion: the inhabitants of cold climates, i. e. the whites, are accuftomed to perpetual exertion: the inhabitants of hot climates, i. e. the blacks, are from their infancy accuftomed to perpetual indolence; for the neceffaries of life in Africa are almoft fpontaneoufly produced; therefore, à fortiori, the whites are the propereft perfons for the labour. Agreeable to this is the fact, that a European conftitution ftands an American climate better than a native. The blackfmiths, carpenters, wheel-wrights, builders, &c. all the trades that require great exertion to perform with fuccefs, are performed by whites, in the Weft-India iflands. A blackfmith, a fmelter, a worker in a glafs-houfe, &c. in this kingdom, work in a more fultry, and a more unwholfome climate than the negroes in in the West-Indies. A gentleman informed me very lately, that his brother, with the other officers of the regiment to which he belonged, in the West Indies, used the daily amusement of *Cricket*. The swampy climate of Georgia is at least equally hot, and certainly more unhealthy, than our West-India islands. " I and my family (says Mr. John Wesley) eight in number, employed all our spare time, while in Georgia, in felling trees and clearing of ground ; as hard labour as any negro need be employed in. The German family, likewise, 40 in number, were employed in all manner of labour. And this was so far from impairing our health, that we all continued perfectly well, while the idle ones round about us were swept away, as with a pestilence." (Thoughts, &c. 20.) 4. If the blacks be manumitted, they must do something for their living: you need not feed them unless they will earn it, and then they will be compelled of themselves to work for you. The Marons and Charibs do not come for employ, because they have been brought up in a state of warfare with the civilized inhabitants ; because they can subsist by hunting or plunder, not being very numerous ; because they have been educated to this mode of life, and it is a known fact, that either white or black thus brought up from his infancy, will never voluntarily settle to regular labour: because they as well as the *free negroes* in the plantations, if they are to work, must work in the gang with the *slaves*, a disgrace which it is well known they will live any how rather than submit to; and because if they were to hire themselves to work in the plantations, they would earn less than they now can do by keeping shop, or as hucksters, &c. for within these few years, gangs might have been hired at 8d. or 10d. a day per head, and during the war, the price did not exceed 13d. ½ but none of these objections would lie to the gradual or even sudden manumission of the numerous negroes now holden in slavery: so that the instances do not, in any degree, countenance the inconveniences dreaded. 5. The Slave-trade, during the war, was almost annihilated ; the consequence was, the slaves became more valuable; and were better treated in some degree; and we do not hear that any enormous inconvenience was the result. 6. But granting that the West-India Islands could not be cultivated without slaves, which is very far from being the case; yet the nation would become very considerably the gainers, by attending to the colonization of Africa, rather than the West-Indies, which will certainly at one time or other involve us in another *American* war. The use of a Colony, is to supply the Mother Country with those commodities which the latter is in want of and can-

not

not produce, at a cheaper rate, and in greater perfection than the Mother Country can be supplied with from any other place: and secondly, to take off those commodities in exchange, which the Colony cannot produce, and which the Mother Country has to spare. For this purpose, the first confideration ought to be, to colonize in an *oppofite* climate: the effect of colonizing in a *fimiliar climate* we have found, by the moft imprudent and abfurd encouragement which we afforded to the *North* American colonies. Wherever therefore the commodities required, can be raifed in the greateft plenty and the greateft perfection, other circumftances being equal, that is the proper place for colonization; and of this, *oppofition of climate* is the firft evidence. Now, it is a notorious fact, that in the hot climate of Africa, every product of our Weft-India Iflands may be produced in much greater abundance, and much higher perfection: Cotton, of various kinds, grows fpontaneoufly: Indigo of the firft quality is indigenous: the fugar-cane in Africa, is 3 or 4 times the fize that we fee it in the Weft-Indies; and they have befide, what the Weft-Indies have not, ivory, and unexplored gold mines. The probable quantity of produce in the colony, is the exponent of the probable quantity of home manufactures, which that colony will take off; for thefe laft can only be paid for by the former. But in Africa, Weft-India products would be produced, not only in greater perfection, but in greater plenty within the fame fpace. But when to this is added, the fuperior extent of fpace, and of fea coaft too; there is the utmoft probability that the colonization of Africa would anfwer to this country far better than that of the Weft-Indies, and the confumption of our manufactures, and of our revenue, would be very confiderably encreafed. Not that in the prefent ftate of things, fuch a colonization not begun, is to be attempted, while an old one remains; but I argue upon the improbable fuppofition that our Weft-Indian colonies would be materially injured by the manumiffion of flaves, and the abolition of the Slave-trade. But that fuch injury would arife, no one can reafonably expect, who confiders, that in the State of Delaware, in America, flavery is abolifhed; that the Quakers have found their intereft in their honefty; and that in confequence of paft experience, the State of Virginia has lately prohibited the importation or purchafe of a flave, under a penalty of 1000l.

IX. But the Slave-trade is a lucrative traffic to this country, and ought therefore to be encouraged.

Anfwer 1. Honefty is the beft policy: no lucre is cheap that is purchafed at the expence of that, which all mankind agree ought never to be expended.

The

The average amount of the exports to Africa, is not above 500,000l. Of what moment, pray, can the profit upon this capital be, when compared with the price paid? 2. But it is a great doubt whether it be lucrative to the nation at all. For the riches of the nation is compoſed of the riches of individuals : the capital of the nation is the aggregate of the capitals of individuals : the gain to the nation upon any particular branch of commerce, is the average gain upon the aggregate of the capitals of the individuals employed in that branch of commerce. But I have heard it repeatedly aſſerted, that for ſome years paſt the African Slave-trade has been carried on to the conſiderable loſs of many individuals employed in it, and that even at preſent, ſucceſs depends not upon the regular events of the trade, but upon ſuch care and conduct in the captains employed, as does not redound to the credit either of them or their employers. 3. It is notorious that the French and Spaniards, who deal largely in ſlaves, conſider the trade as a looſing one ; for a great part of the Slave-trade of this country, *is for the ſupply of the French and Spaniſh colonies.* At the time of Mr. Ramſay's writing, ſome Engliſh ſlave-dealers were treating with the court of Spain, for the regular ſupply of the Spaniſh colonies with 80,000 annual ſlaves. Can that trade be lucrative to this country which ſupplies to the French and Spaniards, the means of cultivating a branch of commerce, wherein they are our rivals?

X. The Slave-trade is a nurſery for ſeamen.

Anſwer. It is the grave of the beſt ſeamen in the Britiſh ſervice.

It is well known, that the ſailors diſlike the trade : that they are frequently kidnapped to enter into it; that they are ill treated in it; and that very many die in it ; far beyond the common proportion. 2. It is well known too, that as more hands are neceſſary to collect ſlaves than to navigate the veſſel ; hence they are ill treated in the mid-voyage, for the owners gain, by their death, their keep and their pay.

Such are the Arguments that have occurred to me on each ſide the Queſtion.

Reader : lay your hand upon your breaſt, and aſk yourſelf ſeriouſly and ſolemnly (for it is a ſolemn buſineſs) the Queſtion, " Is this Traffic, upon the whole, honeſt or diſhoneſt? If the latter ; is it not your duty to ſet your face againſt it, with an earneſtneſs proportionate to the extent and enormity of the evil? Act in this caſe as your conſcience ſhall direct ; the Appeal has been made to you, and at one day or other you will anſwer for your own conduct herein.

This Day is published, in One Volume 8vo. Price 4s. in Boards,

By J. Phillips, George-Yard, Lombard-Street,

An Effay on the Slavery and Commerce of the Human Species, particularly the African, tranflated from a Latin Differtation, which was honoured with the firft Prize in the Univerfity of Cambridge, for the Year 1785, with Additions. By J. Clarkfon. 4s. Boards.

Where may be alfo had, lately publifhed,

A Letter from Capt. J. S. Smith, to the Rev. Mr. Hill, on the State of the Negroe Slaves. To which are added an in - troduction, and Remarks on free Negroes, &c. By the Editor. Price 6d.

Effay on the Treatment and Converfion of African Slaves in the Britifh Sugar Colonies. By the Rev. J. Ramfay, Vicar of Tefton in Kent. 4s. Boards.

An Inquiry into the Effects of putting a Stop to the African Slave Trade, and of granting Liberty to the Slaves in the Britifh Sugar Colonies. By J. Ramfay. Price 6d.

A Reply to the perfonal Invectives and Objections contained in two Anfwers, publifhed by certain anonymous Perfons, to an Effay on the Treatment and Converfion of African Slaves, in the Britifh Colonies. By J. Ramfay. Price 2s.

Thoughts on the Slavery of the Negroes. Price 4d.

A Caution to Great Britain and her Colonies, in a fhort Reprefentation of the calamitous State of the enflaved Negroes in the Britifh Dominions. By Anthony Benezet. Price 6d.

A ferious Addrefs to the Rulers of America, on the Inconfiftency of their Conduct refpecting Slavery. Price 3d.

The Cafe of our Fellow-Creatures, the oppreffed Africans, refpectfully recommended to the ferious Confideration of the Legiflature of Great Britain, by the People called Quakers. Price 2d.

A Defcription of Guinea, its Situation, Produce, and the general Difpofition of its Inhabitants; with an Enquiry into
the

the Rife and progrefs of the Slave Trade, &c. By Anthony
Benezet. Sewed, 2s.

A Fragment on the Slavery of the Negroes. By Day. 1s.
Stockdale.

Wefley's Thoughts on the Slavery of the Negroes. 2d.

G. Sharpe's Law of Liberty. 9d.

———————— Limitation of Slavery. 2s. 6d.

———————— Law of paffive Obedience. 9d.

John Woolinan. Some Effays in his Works.

———

FOR THE SLAVE TRADE.

An Apology for Negro Slavery. Faulder.

Curfory Remarks on Ramfay's Effay. By Tobin. 2s. 6d.
Wilkie.

N. B. Now in the Prefs, an Anfwer to Tobin's Rejoinder.
By Ramfay.

Rejoinder to Ramfay's Reply. By Ditto. 1s. 6d. Wilkie.

The Subject of the Slave Trade is alfo animadverted on, in
a Sermon exprefsly on this topic, among thofe publifhed by
Dr. Porteus, Bifhop of Chefter.

In a Sermon, on the reciprocal Duties of Mafters and Ser-
vants, by Dr. Fofter; vid. Fofter's Sermons, qto. v. 2, p. 156
et feq.

See alfo to the fame purpofe Dodfley's Annual Regifter, v.
15, for the Year 1772, among the Poetry.

Ibid v. 18. p. 173 et feq.

Ibid v. 12, p. 168—209.

Many paffages alfo on this fubject are to be found in Cow-
per's Poems; in the Letters of Ignatius Sancho, &c.

THE END.

www.ingramcontent.com/pod-product-compliance
Lightning Source LLC
Chambersburg PA
CBHW021454090426
42739CB00009B/1748